# DEVELOPING YOUR IDENTITY IN CHRIST

Copyright © 2019 Clifton E. Bright Jr

All Scripture quotations, unless otherwise indicated, are taken from the Amplified Bible (AMPCE), Copyright © 1954, 1958, 1962, 1964, 1965, 1987 by The Lockman Foundation. Used by permission.

Scripture taken from the New King James Version®. Copyright © 1982 by Thomas Nelson. Used by permission. All rights reserved.

ISBN-13: 978-0-9981891-2-3

Printed in the United States of America

# INTRODUCTION

When a car pulls up behind you, do you pull over? More than likely, you don't. Imagine blue lights pulling up behind you, would you pull over then? Probably. You would identify this as a police vehicle and because you are aware of their authority, you would respect it. Your response to this and most situations is based on the way you see certain things. According to the Merriam-Webster dictionary, "identity" means "sameness of essential or generic character in different instances: sameness in all that constitutes the objective reality of a thing: oneness."

In different scenarios, you can identify or recognize what a person or an object represents. For example, you would respond to a random gentleman who steps on your shoe and gets in your face differently than you would respond to Mike Tyson if he were to do the same thing. (Maybe that's just me!) Nevertheless, identity dictates the circumstances in your life. We all identify ourselves in some way: gender, race, economic status, occupation, etc. The limits on a man's life are governed by identity.

When you look at the ills of our society today, men are under attack. Honestly, the man has been under attack since creation. We have generations of men who do not know who they are. According to the Bureau of Justice, more than two million men are incarcerated. Some studies have shown that high school dropout rates have declined because of increases in the prison population. Fathers are essential when establishing the identity of a child. The rate of children growing up

## Introduction

in homes without one is astronomical. According to the United States Census Bureau, 23.6 percent of US children (17.4 million) lived in father absent homes in 2014. The man is the standard bearer in his home...or at least he should be. The absence of a strong male figure from many homes has had negative effects on entire families. Studies have shown that children who do not have a father in their lives have a greater chance of growing up in poverty, a lower chance of academic success, and are more susceptible to being incarcerated. Often, men mimic the identities that they have been taught in their environments, but this can change once a man receives Jesus as Lord and Savior.

A few years ago, I remember running into a close friend who was involved in all kinds of sinful behavior when we were younger. When I saw him that day, I was discouraged and going through a difficult time in my life, and he ministered to me! He had made major changes in his life and was able to encourage me. Let me paint you a picture of this encounter. It was my first day working at a local restaurant. I walked to the grill and I saw my close friend. I said, "What's up" and he replied, "Praise the Lord!" I was floored. He spent that eight-hour shift telling me about how God desires to have a minute-by-minute relationship with us as men. He gave me scripture after scripture to support his points. As men, when we are secure in our identity in Christ, we can be a light for our brothers who are going through trials. Just like the Apostle Paul encouraged his eager mentee Timothy in 1 and 2 Timothy, knowing who you are in Christ can position you to do the same.

As men, when we are whole and complete on the inside and know who we are in Christ, we can be that light for our brothers who are going through challenges. Our spiritual health is not just about us, but it's for those around us as well! Just as the Apostle Paul encouraged his young mentee Timothy in 1 Timothy 4:16, when we pay attention to the spiritual lessons that we're learning, we will not just save ourselves, but our hearers as well.

Over the next twenty-one days, this devotional will begin to develop and/or build your understanding of your identity in Jesus Christ. The purpose of this devotional for men is to encourage and help you develop an understanding of who you are in Christ. The first week deals with man's original identity and what transpired to cause his deception. Satan deceived Eve, and as a byproduct of this occurrence, Adam ate from the Tree of the Knowledge of Good and Evil.

The remaining fourteen days will allow Jesus to restore your identity and to spiritually develop your soul, which consists of your mind, emotions, desires, and feelings. A scripture will accompany each insight regarding the Word's definition of identity. I challenge you with a confession called, "Identify with This" at the end of each day. It has been said many times that confession brings possession. When you verbally declare that something belongs to you (such as deliverance from bondage), it is more likely that it will become a reality in your life. This is a key to enlarge every area of your life: your family, community, and this world! Men, if you are ready to identify who you are in Jesus, let's get started!

# DAY 1

# IT TAKES FAITH!

> (as it is written [in Scripture], "I have made you a father of many nations") in the sight of Him in whom he believed, that is, God who gives life to the dead and calls into being that which does not exist. In hope against hope Abraham believed that he would become a father of many nations, as he had been promised [by God]: "So [numberless] shall your descendants be."
>
> - Romans 4:17-18

When a man receives Jesus Christ as Lord and Savior, he gains a new identity, which is rooted in Christ. He becomes a new being, and this new being is required for man to build, grow, and better understand his purpose. Developing the understanding of identity in Christ is an ongoing process.

At some point, we all struggle to understand who we are in Christ. Faith is the key component to be all God has called you to be. It takes courage to journey beyond who you believe you are. It is important to explore faith in order to gauge God's plan for your life.

What is Faith? Well, Hebrews 11:1 describes faith as the substance of what you hope for and the evidence of things you cannot see. Faith is being in agreement with what God says. Whether you realize it or not, you operate in faith every day. If you walk around scared, defeated, unsure of yourself, paranoid, or hopeless, it is because your faith in the negative words or experiences of your past have distorted your image. It is important to develop the 'God kind of faith' in your life in order to reveal the man God created you to be. This is your true identity.

In the passage above, God promised Abraham a male descendant. He did not see this promise fulfilled until he was one hundred years old and his wife was ninety-nine. God called his heir into being long before he actually showed up. God has called some things into your life that have not shown up yet. Knowing who you are in Him will open the doors for these things to manifest. It takes faith. It takes courage to see yourself as God sees you. You can do it; be encouraged!

# IDENTIFY WITH THIS

Confession: "I am a mighty man of God. I may not feel mighty, and I may not feel like I am of value, but I am. I am valuable because God said I am. I declare that I have faith to be all that God called me to be!"

## DAY 2

# MADE IN HIS IMAGE AND LIKENESS

> Then God said, "Let Us (Father, Son, Holy Spirit) make man in Our image, according to Our likeness [not physical, but a spiritual personality and moral likeness]; and let them have complete authority over the fish of the sea, the birds of the air, the cattle, and over the entire earth, and over everything that creeps and crawls on the earth." So God created man in His own image, in the image and likeness of God He created him; male and female He created them.
>
> - Genesis 1:26-27

Though I have distinct mannerisms, I look just like my mom. My dad and I walk and talk alike, but my personality is my own. If you look at me and my parents, you know I belong to them.

When God made man, He made him in His image—to look like Him and to conduct himself like Him. God did not make man like any of the animals He created. God did not make the animals with an identity rooted in Himself. Only man (which also includes women in this sense) was made in this fashion. God spoke everything He created first, and then it appeared. When God made Adam, God looked at him and declared, "that's mine." So in order to understand your identity and image, you have to become acquainted with who God is and how He conducts Himself. This should eliminate any feelings of worthlessness or low self-esteem. The God who created everything chose to make YOU in His image!

God also gave man complete authority over all He created. That is powerful. This means that God made the earth for man to enjoy, sustain, and direct. He gave us complete dominion over His creation. Think about all the animal fears that consume men: fear of snakes, mice, etc. We were given authority over these animals. Often, it may feel like we have no control over what happens in our lives. Remember that everything has been made for you because of God's love for us. Unfortunately, something happened that took us away from this original image and identity of who we are to God. Deception by Satan caused us to lose our awareness of this image.

A lot of the men I encounter run into great difficulty in life because they do not have an image or identity to pattern themselves after. Subsequently, they have problems understanding the authority they have in their lives. Gaining knowledge and understanding of God's original identity for man can help them.

# IDENTIFY WITH THIS

Confession: "God made me in His image and His likeness, spiritually. I am a man of authority. I am not a no body. I am not just somebody. I am like my Father who is in heaven!"

# DAY 3

# MAN'S FIRST OCCUPATION

> So the Lord God took the man [He had made] and settled him in the Garden of Eden to cultivate and keep it. And the Lord God commanded the man, saying, "You may freely (unconditionally) eat [the fruit] from every tree of the garden; but [only] from the tree of the knowledge (recognition) of good and evil you shall not eat, otherwise on the day that you eat from it, you shall most certainly die [because of your disobedience].
>
> - Genesis 2:15-17

I got my first job when I was sixteen. I worked at the local Golden Corral washing dishes. I remember walking into the back kitchen area and looking at all of the dishes. It was overwhelming. Another guy washing dishes quickly showed me how to work the hose and dishwasher and where to put the dishes after washing them. He demonstrated one cycle of the process and walked away leaving me on my own. Needless to say, that first night was a long one. I felt like I did not know what I was doing at first, but this caused me to have a greater understanding of my duties.

God put man (Adam) in the garden and gave him a job: to cultivate the garden and keep it. Merriam-Webster defines "cultivate" as "to foster growth of, to improve by labor, care and study." Adam was supposed to improve and grow what God created. God identified man as a cultivator.

God originally designed us to improve places, people, and situations that we are a part of. We are not to cause things to reduce, shrink, or worsen. Gaining an understanding of this aspect of your identity will cause things to change in your life, home, and community.

You may ask yourself, "As a man, am I causing the places, people, and situations in my life to grow?" If the answer is yes, understand there is still more room to grow as you continue to refine your identity. If the answer is no, getting an understanding of who you are in Christ can turn that around for you.

# IDENTIFY WITH THIS

Confession: "God has made me a cultivator. I cause things to improve and grow. I take care of responsibilities that are under my care. Anything that touches my hands leaves in better condition and expands for its good. I cultivate positive growth in myself, my family and friends, and in my community."

## Man's First Occupation

# DAY 4

# IDENTITY CAUSES RECOGNITION

Now the Lord God said, "It is not good (beneficial) for the man to be alone; I will make him a helper [one who balances him—a counterpart who is] [i]suitable and complementary for him." So the Lord God formed out of the ground every animal of the field and every bird of the air, and brought them to Adam to see what he would call them; and whatever the man called a living creature, that was its name. And the man gave names to all the livestock, and to the birds of the air, and to every animal of the field; but for Adam there was not found a helper [that was] suitable (a companion) for him. So the Lord God caused a deep sleep to fall upon Adam; and while he slept, He took one of his ribs and closed up the flesh at that place. And the rib which the Lord God had taken from the man He made (fashioned, formed) into a woman, and He brought her and presented her to the man. Then Adam said, "This is now bone of my bones, And flesh of my flesh; She shall be called Woman, Because she was taken out of Man.

- Genesis 3:18-23

God knows what you need even when you do not have a clue. In this case, He knew Adam needed someone to help him. He needed someone to balance his work life. God brought all the animals to the man to name and in naming them, Adam did not find a help meet (or companion) for himself. So God took a rib from the man and made the woman. Adam identified her as his helpmate.

I remember when God first started dealing with me about my wife before we were married. I had given up on getting married at the time and was fine with being single for the rest of my life. He started showing me some of the qualities I would need in a helpmate.

Whether in marriage or business, God will provide what you need to complete your assignment. You have to recognize your help when it is presented to you. Identifying your purpose opens the door for you to recognize when provision comes. As my wife and I go on year to year, we continue to recognize why God put us together.

You may be at a place where you think you are in a deficit or have no direction. Understanding your identity and purpose will open your eyes to the opportunities God has put in place for you.

# IDENTIFY WITH THIS

Confession: "God made me in His image. I have power in my tongue. I call circumstances, situations, and people what He calls them in His Word. Whatever I need, He will provide from sources I cannot even begin to come up with."

## Identity Causes Recognition

## DAY 5

# A LACK OF IDENTITY LEADS TO DECEPTION

> Now the serpent was more crafty (subtle, skilled in deceit) than any living creature of the field which the Lord God had made. And the serpent (Satan) said to the woman, "Can it really be that God has said, 'You shall not eat from any tree of the garden'?" And the woman said to the serpent, "We may eat fruit from the trees of the garden, except the fruit from the tree which is in the middle of the garden. God said, 'You shall not eat from it nor touch it, otherwise you will die.'" But the serpent said to the woman, "You certainly will not die! For God knows that on the day you eat from it your eyes will be opened [that is, you will have greater awareness], and you will be like God, knowing [the difference between] good and evil." And when the woman saw that the tree was good for food, and that it was delightful to look at, and a tree to be desired in order to make one wise and insightful, she took some of its fruit and ate it; and she also gave some to her husband with her, and he ate. Then the eyes of the two of them were opened [that is, their awareness increased], and they knew that they were naked; and they fastened fig leaves together and made themselves coverings.
>
> - Genesis 3:1- 7

Let's revisit the instructions about the tree. Once you identify who you are, then there are guidelines and principles that go with that identity. When I was a dishwasher, I had to adhere to the standards that were put in place for those who were dishwashers. It did not matter if I measured up to the standards of the prep cook. That was not my identity and purpose at the restaurant. Understand that we should not measure ourselves against others, whether in accomplishments, looks, education, or other areas. Jesus should be the measuring stick we use to evaluate ourselves.

Eve was told by Adam that they were not to eat from the Tree of the Knowledge of Good and Evil, yet she let Satan talk her into doing so. Satan deceived her because she was uncertain about her identity. Adam was ultimately responsible for making sure she knew her identity. Satan told her that if she ate from the tree she would have been just like God. The problem is that this was a lie. Eve didn't realize that she was already as close to God's likeness as she could have possibly been. God had already told Adam that He was made in His image and likeness. Satan essentially convinced Eve to forfeit her destiny and position in exchange for a false reality. If you are not sure of who you are, anyone can talk you into the wrong thing or talk you out of what belongs to you.

When I was in third grade, I beat up my best friend. I did it to impress a girl that I liked. She could not stand him and asked me to punch him. I figured I would get in good with her since, on my own, I didn't seem to be good enough. I ended up getting rejected by her anyway and I lost a friend. This was deception at its finest. Ask yourself, "What is lacking in my awareness of my identity and what is it costing me?"

The biggest issue that comes out of this serpent

situation for Adam and Eve is that Adam missed a part of his purpose. He was supposed to take care of everything in the garden and protect it. He sat there and let a snake talk to his wife.

Notice your position men: nothing negative occurred in the garden until man ate the fruit. God had already told Adam what his purpose was. He had a responsibility to protect the woman from deception and he failed to do so. Anytime you fail to do so in areas of your life, you allow deception to weaken what God has already built within you.

A Lack of Identity Leads to Deception

# IDENTIFY WITH THIS

**Confession: "I know who I am. I cannot be deceived because I continually meditate and focus on who I am in Christ."**

## A Lack of Identity Leads to Deception

# DAY 6

# LACK OF IDENTITY BRINGS FEAR

> And they heard the sound of the Lord God walking in the garden in the cool [afternoon breeze] of the day, so the man and his wife hid and kept themselves hidden from the presence of the Lord God among the trees of the garden. But the Lord God called to Adam, and said to him, "Where are you?" He said, "I heard the sound of You [walking] in the garden, and I was afraid because I was naked; so I hid myself." God said, "Who told you that you were naked? Have you eaten [fruit] from the tree of which I commanded you not to eat?
>
> - Genesis 3:8-11

When I was growing up in Philadelphia, I had an older friend who took me under his wing. Let's call him Bob. When Bob was around, I had confidence in what I did and said. If someone got smart with me, I knew they could not beat Bob. When I saw a girl I liked, if Bob was around, I would talk to her. When he moved away, so did my confidence.

Confidence was one of the attributes Adam lost when he was disobedient. Adam realized he was naked, because he was no longer covered by God. When this happened, the man became afraid and he hid. When you do not know who you are, you will run and hide from situations. Satan infiltrated Adam and Eve's image and caused them to exchange their authority with his. He has done the same to a lot of men in this world.

At the time, I thought that Bob's departure was one of the worst things that could have happened to me. However, it actually caused me to grow into who I am today. I had to learn to overcome fear on my own. Discovering identity will cause you to persevere and relinquish the spirit of fear. You may be afraid because of what you see when you look into your metaphorical mirror. You cannot identify who you are or the path you are supposed to take. This is in God's control. When you begin to see yourself in the image that God created you, you will be courageous and confident.

# IDENTIFY WITH THIS

Confession: "God covers me. I honor Him and reverence Him. He wants me to know who I am in Him and to not let another voice distract me."

## Lack of Identity Brings Fear

# DAY 7

# THE PERVERSION OF OUR IDENTITY

Then to Adam the Lord God said, "Because you have listened [attentively] to the voice of your wife, and have eaten [fruit] from the tree about which I commanded you, saying, 'You shall not eat of it'; The ground is [now] under a curse because of you; In sorrow and toil you shall eat [the fruit] of it All the days of your life." Both thorns and thistles it shall grow for you; And you shall eat the plants of the field. "By the sweat of your face You will eat bread Until you return to the ground, For from it you were taken; For you are dust, And to dust you shall return.

- Genesis 3:17-19

The word "perversion" in the Merriam Webster Dictionary is defined as, "the alteration of something from its original course, meaning, or state to a distortion or corruption of what was first intended." Satan was able to pervert Adam's authority and purpose by convincing Adam to go against his own identity which was made in the image of God. This disobedience caused the ground to become corrupted. The man who was designed to be a cultivator now had to work the ground with sorrow to get anything from it. Instead of living forever in paradise, God told the man he would return to dust.

Perhaps someone said the wrong thing to you

as a child, mistreated you, and took advantage of you. They may have perverted your identity by saying negative words to you about your future. They may have disregarded your value. Your life (which was originally designed to prosper) may now be going in the wrong direction. Learning who you are in Christ will cause you to plant seeds that produce, for you and for His glory. Your obedience to Him will keep your identity from becoming distorted and prevent you from going off course.

# IDENTIFY WITH THIS

Confession: "I am willing and obedient, therefore I eat the good of the land. I am not operating under the curse. I am blessed (empowered to prosper). Everything my hand touches prospers."

# The Perversion of Our Identity

## DAY 8

# THE HOPE OF RENEWED IDENTITY

> And I will put enmity (open hostility) between you and the woman, And between your seed (offspring) and her Seed; He shall [fatally] bruise your head, And you shall [only] bruise His heel.
>
> - Genesis 3:15

God told the serpent that the woman's offspring (or seed) would fatally bruise his head. The seed is Jesus. He bruised the enemy's head on the cross, the same place Satan bruised Jesus' heel. Jesus is the one who reconciled us to our original identity and purpose. It looked like Satan had won. He had Adam and Eve put out of the Garden and the man had lost his original identity and intent. There is an identity that God has designated for you before the foundation of the world. Your true, God-given identity is wrestling with the identity the world has tried to put on you.

It doesn't matter where you are right now, this Word is for you. It was given centuries before Jesus' sacrifice crushed the work of Satan. You are who God says you are according to His Word. If you will commit yourself to studying what He says about you and let it get into your soul, it will transform your life forever. It will drive fear out of your life and will cause you to soar into everything God has called you into.

# IDENTIFY WITH THIS

Confession: "No matter where I am right now in life, there is more for me to discover about my identity. Jesus is my hope and He dwells inside me. I am never without hope and a future."

## The Hope of Renewed Identity

# DAY 9

# YOU'VE ALWAYS BEEN WHO GOD CREATED YOU TO BE

> In the beginning [before all time] was the Word (Christ), and the Word was with God, and the Word was God Himself. He was [continually existing] in the beginning [co-eternally] with God. But to as many as did receive and welcome Him, He gave the right [the authority, the privilege] to become children of God, that is, to those who believe in (adhere to, trust in, and rely on) His name.
>
> - John 1:1-2, 12

Before time even became a factor, Jesus was here. Jesus represents the Word that was spoken when God formed creation. When Jesus showed up on the earth in the form of a man, He came to those who were perceived to be God's people. Unfortunately, the Pharisees and other Jewish leaders rejected Him because they didn't see Him as the Messiah (more on this later). He called those who accepted Him the children of God. Through Him, our identity changed from being outcasts to belonging to God. God's acceptance of us through Jesus shattered all of the religious expectations of that time.

If you have ever experienced rejection, you know

it makes you feel like there is nothing good in you. I remember when I was in the sixth grade I got rejected by an eighth-grader who was the most popular girl in school. This experience scarred me and, for years, made me believe that I had nothing to offer anyone else. You may feel that way right now, but understand that Jesus has given you the privilege of being a child of God. There is nothing about you that is unworthy. God created you and granted you an identity. Your continual fellowship with Him will draw out the greatness that God put in you from the beginning.

# IDENTIFY WITH THIS

Confession: "God had a plan for me from the beginning and now I am a Child of God through receiving Jesus as Lord and Savior. I am not a reject. I am valuable!"

# DAY 10

# IDENTITY PRECEDES WORK

> After Jesus was baptized, He came up immediately out of the water, and behold, the heavens were opened, and he (John) saw the Spirit of God descending as a dove and lighting on Him (Jesus), and behold, a voice from heaven said, "This is My beloved Son, in whom I am well-pleased and delighted!"
>
> - Matthew 3:16-17

Jesus went through the process of getting baptized before He went into full-time ministry. God placed an anointing on Him and then told Him his identity. He told Him that He was pleased and delighted in Him! All of this occurred before Jesus entered into full-time ministry.

How many of us, as men, yearn to hear this from our fathers? I know I did for years. Some do not have the opportunity to hear that from their fathers because many men pass away before saying those words to their sons. Up until the age of forty, I expected my father to look at me and say, "good job," every time I accomplished anything. It was around that time that he told me he was proud of me. Hearing those words sent a shot of adrenaline through me! It added confidence to my efforts and my perception of myself elevated. How much more will God's approval of us elevate our thinking and identity? As men (especially fathers) we have the ability to cause our children, spouses, and others to expand their lives. Let's not take this lightly!

# IDENTIFY WITH THIS

Confession: "My Heavenly Father approved me and is interested in my future. He wants to prepare me for the work He has laid out for me and His Love for me strengthens me to handle anything."

## Identity Precedes Work

# DAY 11

# IDENTITY CAN WITHSTAND TEMPTATION

> Then Jesus was led by the Spirit into the wilderness to be tempted by the devil. After fasting forty days and forty nights, he was hungry. The tempter came to him and said, "If you are the Son of God, tell these stones to become bread."
> Jesus answered, "It is written: 'Man shall not live on bread alone, but on every word that comes from the mouth of God.
>
> - Matthew 4:1-4 (NKJV)

The devil attempted to challenge Jesus in the area of identity. When Satan began his interrogation of Jesus, three times in this chapter, he said, "If thou be..." He was saying this to test if Jesus was aware of His identity. It is easy to fall into temptation based on who you perceive yourself to be. Jesus used the Word to put Satan in his place!

I remember how a situation in the sixth grade caused me to have low self-esteem. I had written a note to the prettiest girl in school with checkboxes asking her out. Instead of keeping it between us, she broadcasted it to everyone willing to listen. She did this while laughing at me with others. This caused me to think I was ugly and to become reluctant to approach any girl for many years. When I did summon the courage to approach one, I portrayed myself as someone I was not.

Satan attacks (or tempts) us in various areas to keep us from functioning as we should. Whether it's the beautiful woman at the gym, the secretary at work, or the ability to cut corners in business, we are surrounded by temptation. Knowing who you are based on what God says in His Word and standing on it will drive any attack away from your presence. When he strikes your supposed weakness, who you are in Christ will stand.

# IDENTIFY WITH THIS

Confession: "I am fearfully and wonderfully made by God! I refuse to settle for anything in life that does not line up with what my Daddy says about me!"

## Identity can Withstand Temptation

# DAY 12

# IDENTITY DETERMINES MY WORDS

Whoever rejects Me and refuses to accept My teachings, has one who judges him; the very word that I spoke will judge and condemn him on the last day. For I have never spoken on My own initiative or authority, but the Father Himself who sent Me has given Me a commandment regarding what to say and what to speak.

- John 12:48-49

For the words which You gave me I have given to them: and they have received and accepted them.

- John 17:8

To operate in this new identity, you and I have to know how to speak. Remember we are looking at Jesus and the example He has set for us to walk in this identity. Jesus stated that He never said anything that God did not tell Him to say. He learned how to operate in the identity of the Son of God through what was spoken to Him. Likewise, our words demonstrate who we are and how we've grown. Jesus even stated that the Father gave Him a commandment, an order of what to say.

Think about the words you speak regularly. Do they align with the identity that God gave to you? Or did your words develop through your experiences and the words you have heard? Are you speaking words that you received from the guys you've hung out with? Locker room talk? Did they come from your father or uncles? Those words may not be kingdom words. One of the regular challenges I run into in my career is helping people overcome the negative words which shaped who they are. Growing up, many people were told that they were nobodies, losers, ugly, fat, worthless. The words we hear and speak are bricks that construct our self-image. When you spend time in the Word, you will fill yourself with words of life and an identity derived from Christ. Contrarily, if you neglect to spend time in the Word, you will lessen the effectiveness of your God-given identity.

# IDENTIFY WITH THIS

Confession: "I may have heard words in the past that have affected how I see myself. I now choose to believe my identity as it has been ordained by the Word of God. I am a winner. I am valuable. I am worth everything to God. He has shown this by what Jesus did on the cross for me."

## Identity Determines My Words

## DAY 13

# IDENTITY BRINGS AUTHORITY

> Love has been perfected among us in this: that we may have boldness in the day of judgment; because as He is, so are we in this world.
>
> - 1 John 4:17 (NKJV)

> Behold, I give you the authority to trample on serpents and scorpions, and over all the power of the enemy, and nothing shall by any means hurt you. Nevertheless do not rejoice in this, that the spirits are subject to you, but rather rejoice because your names are written in heaven.
>
> - Luke 10:19-20 (NKJV)

This newfound identity comes with an authority that you did not have before: the authority to handle any situation that shows up in your life. Serpents and scorpions mentioned in Luke 10:19-20 represent some of the cunning trials, attacks and issues sent by Satan that come to plague us in the human experience. Through this passage, Jesus told us not to get excited about the power to overcome life situations, but to get excited that our names are written in heaven. This means that you and I are not going to hell anymore and we can operate in boldness.

Have you ever been in a situation where you felt like you had no right to say anything? No power to change your situation? Understand that because of who you are in Christ, you have the authority to overcome any situation. His love should give us boldness. Sometimes, I deal with thoughts in my mind contrary to who God says I am. Those thoughts can get so loud that they beat me down. We have authority to run those thoughts off by reminding them of who we are! Man of God, this world needs you to know who you are and it needs you to walk in your authority.

# IDENTIFY WITH THIS

Confession: "I don't have to submit to thoughts from the enemy or my past. I have authority over the power of the devil because of who I am in Jesus Christ. I refuse to allow anything to stay in my life that is the opposite of my identity!

# DAY 14

# IDENTITY CAUSES PERSEVERANCE

> And after going a little farther, He fell face down and prayed, saying, "My Father, if it is possible [that is, consistent with Your will], let this cup pass from Me; yet not as I will, but as You will." ... He went away a second time and prayed, saying, "My Father, if this cannot pass away unless I drink it, Your will be done." Again He came and found them sleeping, for their eyes were heavy. So, leaving them again, He went away and prayed for the third time, saying the same words once more.
>
> - Matthew 26:39, 42-44

At times in life you may just want to quit. Everyone has these moments when they want to give up. Matthew 26 presents a moment when Jesus wanted to give up. He asked the Father three times if He could let the cup which represented Him dying on the cross pass from Him... but only if it was aligned with the Father's will. Jesus' identity was conformed to the will of God. This truth caused Him to persevere in the midst of probably the hardest moment any man has faced.

On a daily basis, it seems that I run into a situation where I want to say, "Let this cup pass, Lord." I am pretty sure you can relate. I have to make a decision based on the identity of who I am in Christ to persevere. In this world, men are quitting daily. Men walk out on their marriages and children, quit jobs, and stop pursuing their dreams. This does not have to be your destiny. God gave you and I the power to make decisions. He made us free moral agents, meaning He does not force us to obey the Word. You and I must decide to follow instruction. In Hebrews, it states that the Father heard Jesus when He prayed. Jesus could have refused to take the cup, but that would have been bad for you and I. So when challenges arise, don't quit. Remind those challenges of who you are in Christ. Sickness? I am healed! Money problems? My God provides! Depression? The joy of the Lord is my strength!

# IDENTIFY WITH THIS

Confession: "I refuse to quit. I no longer identify with quitting because Jesus does not. I can speak to every negative situation and it will have to line up with my identity which is found in the Word of God!"

## Identity Causes Perseverance

# DAY 15

# THE FINAL PAYMENT FOR YOUR IDENTITY

> And Jesus cried out again with a loud [agonized] voice, and gave up His spirit [voluntarily, sovereignly dismissing and releasing His spirit from His body in submission to His Father's plan].
>
> - Matthew 27:50

There it is. Jesus on the cross. He made the final payment so that you and I could identify as God's children. Understand this truth: because Jesus rose three days later, your new identity is sealed in Him. We can never repay Him for His awesome sacrifice. He died for your sins and mine. Nothing can change this. He did this willingly. How many people are willing to die for those they love?

As a parent of three, there is no question that I would give my life for my children. Not many would give their lives for strangers, especially those who are considered to be enemies. Jesus prayed on the cross for the people who had put Him there. Praying for those who have wronged me has been a challenge for me in the past. I had to accept that this is a part of our identity and responsibility in Christ.

Ask yourself this question: what would you voluntarily give up for God? This is a daily aspect of growing in your identity. As a man, sometimes you want to get back at someone instead of praying for them. Let your new identity reign.

# IDENTIFY WITH THIS

Confession: "Thank you, Jesus, for giving your life for me. You did not have to do it, but you did it, because you love me. Show me what I may need to release in order to operate in my identity in you."

# The Final Payment for your Identity

# DAY 16

# YOU ARE RIGHTEOUS

> He made Christ who knew no sin to [judicially] be sin on our behalf, so that in Him we would become the righteousness of God [that is, we would be made acceptable to Him and placed in a right relationship with Him by His gracious lovingkindness].
>
> - 2 Corinthians 5:21

An important aspect to understand about your identity in Christ is that you are righteous. You did not work your way to becoming identified as righteous. You were made righteous by your acceptance of Jesus' death, burial, and resurrection. If you do not get this into your soul, you will be moved by anything that comes your way. Trying to prove your righteousness to God and others will cause you to enter into self-righteousness.

Righteousness is being in good standing with God. This means there is no barrier in your relationship with Him thanks to Jesus. The Word states in Isaiah 64:6, "that our righteousness is as filthy rags." You could never do enough to be right with God. Jesus did it for you. You were in a relationship with the Father once you received Jesus.

When I first became saved, I compared the sins I

struggled with to other people's issues. For instance, I was struggling with lust, but would say things like, "At least I don't use drugs." This is where self-righteousness comes into play. You are not right because you read the Bible for six hours a day, pray for seven hours, and attend every single service your ministry conducts. Some righteous works should stem from these acts, but you are not made right by them. You will never be more right with God than you were the moment you received Jesus. Understand that Jesus removed the curse of the law. The curse of the law was that man could never be justified by the law because he could not keep them all. Breaking one law meant they were guilty of them all. This is why we needed a Savior in the first place. Our power could not get the job done. As a man, it is hard at times to admit you do not have the ability to get a job done. Jesus empowered us through His victory on the cross to be all God called us to be.

# IDENTIFY WITH THIS

Confession: "I AM THE RIGHTEOUSNESS OF GOD IN CHRIST JESUS! My standing with the Father is set. I am justified by Jesus' actions and my God accepts me as one of His own.

## You are Righteous

## DAY 17

# DON'T SEEK STUFF; SEEK THE KINGDOM

> But FIRST and MOST importantly seek (aim at, strive after) His kingdom and His righteousness [His way of doing and being right—the attitude and character of God], and all these things will be given to you also.
>
> - Matthew 6:33 (emphasis mine)

> Simon Peter, a bond-servant and apostle (special messenger, personally chosen representative) of Jesus Christ, to those who have received and possess [by God's will] a precious faith of the same kind as ours, by the righteousness of our God and Savior, Jesus Christ: Grace and peace [that special sense of spiritual well-being] be multiplied to you in the [true, intimate] knowledge of God and of Jesus our Lord. For His divine power has bestowed on us [absolutely] everything necessary for [a dynamic spiritual] life and godliness, through true and personal knowledge of Him who called us by His own glory and excellence. For by these He has bestowed on us His precious and magnificent promises [of inexpressible value], so that by them you may escape from the immoral freedom that is in the world because of disreputable desire, and become sharers of the divine nature.
>
> - 2 Peter 1:1-4

These last few days will focus on some necessary truths that you need to grow and maximize your identity. Let's focus on the source for your life. A person lives their life based on who they think they are. Now that we've established that you are righteous, you need to focus on God's way of doing things. This world is full of people who are seeking things for themselves and coming up with ways to obtain them. God has placed in you the tools to operate the way He does. The more you get to know Him, the more you get to know who you are now.

I think about things I struggled with for years and just could not seem to shake. As I continued to draw closer to God through His Word and prayer, the more I saw those issues start to fall out of my life. This is the result of the precious promises given in the Word. Like the bodybuilder in the gym, the more he engages with weights, the stronger he gets and his muscles become more developed. This is the same with us. If you seek God's way of doing things, you do not have to stoop to the ways that others have to seek success. I know this can be a challenge at times as a man.

In the book, Wild at Heart, Author John Eldredge spoke of how a man will often pursue exploits such as doing well in business to hide his insecurities. You may find yourself seeking things to make you feel more masculine. Seeking the kingdom of God will reveal true manhood to you. The kingdom of God is His system of doing things. Through it, you will learn how to be like your big brother Jesus, who described Himself as the "Firstborn of many brethren." Jesus is our true example of manhood and growing in your identity in Him reveals that manhood. You won't have to seek earthly things to feel manly, operating in God's will uncovers your true manhood.

# IDENTIFY WITH THIS

Prayer: "I no longer do things in my life my way. I, now, decide to seek God's way. I identify myself as a kingdom citizen and I now refuse to operate my old way. Holy Spirit, show me your ways so I can prosper. In Jesus' name, Amen."

# DAY 18

# I HAVE THE SAME MIND AS JESUS

Have this same attitude in yourselves which was in Christ Jesus [look to Him as your example in selfless humility], who, although He existed in the form and unchanging essence of God [as One with Him, possessing the fullness of all the divine attributes—the entire nature of deity], did not regard equality with God a thing to be grasped or asserted [as if He did not already possess it, or was afraid of losing it]; but emptied Himself [without renouncing or diminishing His deity, but only temporarily giving up the outward expression of divine equality and His rightful dignity] by assuming the form of a bond-servant, and being made in the likeness of men [He became completely human but was without sin, being fully God and fully man]. After He was found in [terms of His] outward appearance as a man [for a divinely-appointed time], He humbled Himself [still further] by becoming obedient [to the Father] to the point of death, even death on a cross.

- Philippians 2:5-8

For who has known the mind and purposes of the Lord, so as to instruct Him? But we have the mind of Christ [to be guided by His thoughts and purposes].

- 1 Corinthians 2:16

In order to walk in this newness of identity, you have to have new thoughts. Your mind must be renewed.

How does one go about doing so? Here are a few tips:
1. You must spend time in the Word daily
2. You must monitor what you expose your eyes and ears to.
3. You need to get around like-minded people, especially those who can mentor you.
4. You must make a definite decision to renew your mind.

Christians have the mind of Christ implanted in us when we are saved. Spending time in the Word draws it out more and more. Not having the right mindset can block you from all that belongs to you. For instance, when I was a freshman in high school, I had about three total outfits that I would mix and match in a rotation.

There was a senior who I liked, but I thought that my appearance would keep her from being interested in me. I happened to talk to her about six years later and she stated that she liked me when I was a freshman but I never showed interest. If you do not change your thinking after claiming your new identity in Christ, you will never operate in the fullness of God.

# IDENTIFY WITH THIS

Confession: "I have the same mind that is in Christ Jesus. I am renewing my mind daily and I am committed to this new mind. I am ready to work."

# I Have The Same Mind As Jesus

## DAY 19

# FEAR TOLERATED IS FAITH AND IDENTITY CONTAMINATED

> For God did not give us a spirit of timidity or cowardice or fear, but [He has given us a spirit] of power and of love and of sound judgment and personal discipline [abilities that result in a calm, well-balanced mind and self-control].
>
> - 2 Timothy 1:7

Man of God, Your Father's intention was not for you to be overcome by a spirit of fear. You may be reading this saying, "I have all kinds of fear." Know that it is not from your Father. He gave you a spirit of love, power, and boldness to overcome fear. Fear comes from Satan who has been trying to keep you from operating in your true identity. You hear people say things like, "A little fear is good," or "Everybody is scared of something." That "little fear" is a seed. It opens the door for negative circumstances to come into your life. It drives physical and mental health ailments such as high blood pressure and anxiety. Fear's purpose is to contaminate your faith. 1 John

4:18 states that, "perfect love cast out all fear." In this text, "perfect" means mature. The way to mature in this life of no fear is to spend time in communion with love. GOD IS LOVE and He is His Word. Time spent meditating on the Word, drives out all fear. In today's world, the spirit of fear seems to infiltrate every arena: families, politics and government, workplaces, malls, movie theatres, etc. At all times, refuse to tolerate fear and speak the WORD only.

# IDENTIFY WITH THIS

Confession: "God, you did not give me a spirit of fear. I refuse to fear. I am a faith man. I know you always come through for me. I know I win in every situation because of who I am in Christ!

## Fear Tolerated Is Faith And Identity Contaminated

## DAY 20

# THE MORE YOU GET, THE MORE HE'LL GIVE

> For to everyone who has [and values his blessings and gifts from God, and has used them wisely], more will be given, and [he will be richly supplied so that] he will have an abundance; but from the one who does not have [because he has ignored or disregarded his blessings and gifts from God], even what he does have will be taken away. And throw out the worthless servant into the outer darkness; in that place [of grief and torment] there will be weeping [over sorrow and pain] and grinding of teeth [over distress and anger].
>
> - Matthew 25:29-30

> But you shall remember [with profound respect] the Lord your God, for it is He who is giving you power to make wealth, that He may confirm His covenant which He swore (solemnly promised) to your fathers, as it is this day.
>
> - Deuteronomy 8:18

God has no problem revealing to you the aspects of the kingdom. As a matter of fact, He wants you to grab as much as you can. The more revelation you get and act on (if you don't walk it out, you don't truly have it), the more He'll give to you. As you walk in what He reveals to you, He'll reveal even more.

Why? He desires to establish His Kingdom in this earth. He has blessed you to be a blessing. Blessing means "empowered to prosper." Man of God, growing in your identity will not only benefit you but it will benefit a great many people who come in contact with you. There are people God has placed in our lives in order to touch theirs.

You are His representative, His ambassador on this earth. Part of our identity is to conduct His affairs on this earth. Look at the world and you will see why it is necessary for you to be the man you are called to be!

# IDENTIFY WITH THIS

Confession: "I am one of God's representatives on this earth. The more I seek Him, the more He reveals who He is and who I am in Him. I am ready and willing to hear your voice, Lord, and touch the lives of who you have called me to."

# The More You Get, the More He'll Give

## DAY 21

# IDENTITY BEFORE CONQUEST

> Then the Lord spoke to Moses, saying, "Send men to spy out the land of Canaan, which I am going to give to the sons of Israel." Then Caleb quieted the people before Moses, and said, "Let us go up at once and take possession of it; for we will certainly conquer it." But the men who had gone up with him said, "We are not able to go up against the people [of Canaan], for they are too strong for us."
>
> So they gave the Israelites a bad report about the land which they had spied out, saying, "The land through which we went, in spying it out, is a land that devours its inhabitants. And all the people that we saw in it are men of great stature. There we saw the Nephilim (the sons of Anak are part of the Nephilim); and we were like grasshoppers in our own sight, and so we were in their sight.
>
> - **Numbers 13:1, 30-33 (NKJV)**

Everything you have absorbed these past twenty days leads to this: **how you see yourself will determine what you have and how your life plays out.** Picture the scenario described above. The Lord told Moses that the land of Canaan belonged to the Israelites and told him to send twelve spies to see the land. Ten of the spies saw what was before them and were terrified. Not only that, but they also scared everyone except for two in their camp by their words.

The two, Caleb and Joshua, said, "Let's go take it." The ten were afraid because of their own self-identity. They saw themselves as grasshoppers. That's okay if you are taking on fleas, but they saw the giants in the land. They even assumed that the people in that land saw them as grasshoppers. They had no way to be sure. No one in that land confirmed those views. They had no conversation with the people in Canaan. Why weren't Joshua and Caleb afraid? They believed what God said about them and had to have pondered on it daily. There is so much power contained in the belief and confession of a man!

Writing this devotional was a challenge for me. For a long time, I felt that I had never had anything significant to say. It has taken a great deal of time pondering and confessing what God says about me to create the momentum to engage in this endeavor. My prayer for you, man of God, is that you are empowered to take the possession of your land and your identity in Christ. Nothing can stop you because God has already given you the ability. You must now tap into it and face the giants in your life that have been holding you at bay. You, alone, decide if you are the conqueror or the conquered. God has already made His decision. Romans 8:37 states that you are more than a conqueror. Keep developing in this truth today!

# IDENTIFY WITH THIS

Confession: "I agree with how God sees me. He sees me as more than a conqueror. He has commanded me to take the land, whatever He has called me into; and to conquer. I come into agreement with that today. I am not a grasshopper. I am a giant slayer in Christ! I slay giants in my family life, in my career and business, and in my personal life. My life is a blessing to every person I come in contact with."

# PRAYER OF SALVATION

God so loved the world that He gave His only Son for us. That Son is Jesus Christ and He is the outward expression of God's love for us. In order to partake of the new identity described in this devotional, you must first receive Jesus Christ as your Lord and Savior. He died on the cross for you and I not only to wash away our sins, but to remove the stronghold that sin had on us and make us free in Him. He died and rose again three days later to provide this new identity for us: from sinners on our way to hell to saints saved by the Grace of God. If you have not received Jesus as Lord and Savior and are ready to, pray the following out loud:

> Heavenly Father, I come to You in the Name of Jesus. Your Word says, "Whosoever shall call on the name of the Lord shall be saved" (Acts 2:21). I am calling on You. I pray and ask Jesus to come into my heart and be Lord over my life according to Romans 10:9-10 which states: "That if thou shalt confess with thy mouth the Lord Jesus, and shalt believe in thine heart that God hath raised him from the dead, thou shalt be saved. For with the heart man believeth unto righteousness; and with the mouth confession is made unto salvation." I do that now. I confess that Jesus is Lord, and I believe in my heart that God raised Him from the dead. I am reborn! I am a Christian, a child of the King and a mighty man of God!!

> **Welcome to the family and your new identity, Brother!**

Made in the USA
Monee, IL
11 January 2021